For my dad for teaching me
that our dyslexia is a gift,
and my mom for giving me the
strength to overcome all obstacles.

You cannot spot the dyslexic person in a crowd. You cannot tell that when they read, the letters they see jump around and form new words. You cannot tell that when they work on math problems, the numbers scramble themselves.

Dyslexia is a brain-based learning disability that means you have trouble processing words or numbers. Dyslexia is not a disease, nor is it contagious. Anyone can have dyslexia. It does not matter how athletic, intelligent, artistic, well educated, or funny you are. It is not something to be ashamed of; it is just something you are born with. It may be passed down through families.

My reading problems started when I was four. I was taking piano lessons, but I just could not get the hang of it. The letters and notes I saw blurred and moved around on the music sheets.

The same thing happened when I looked at my books. I felt as though I was reading the Declaration of Independence in Greek. My parents just thought I was goofing off.

That August, I started Kindergarten. My reading problems continued. I also had a tough time with numbers. When my teacher quizzed me verbally, I knew the answers. Still, I struggled to keep pace with everyone else in reading and math because I had to decipher what was written, even though I knew what it meant.

Things did not get easier in first grade. Hannah, my younger sister, was reading at a faster pace than I was at that time. My mom went to the library to borrow alphabet books. We sat together every night and I

would read aloud to her - slowly. While I struggled to sound something out, Hannah stood behind the couch and said the word before I could!

Finally, after another failed attempt at reading Dr. Seuss's *Fox in Socks*, I cried in my mom's lap. I explained to her that the blurry letters kept bouncing around on the page and forming new words.

The word "the" was one of the worst. I saw it - and pronounced it - as "teh." I asked her what was wrong with me.

My mom's eyes grew wide and she became quiet. She carefully told me that I was dyslexic. Dyslexia is a

brain-based learning disorder that makes it hard for children to spell, read, write, and complete math problems.

"Let's try something new," she said. "I have a great idea."

That weekend, when my mom and I went to the library, we headed straight to the section that had children's books on tape. I was amazed by the number of available choices. Mom said that I should borrow both the recorded version and the printed version of the same book. That way, I could read along on the page while listening to the words.

I picked Thomas Rockwell's *How to Eat Fried Worms* as my first adventure. It was easier than I thought it would be to follow along with the narrator's voice. This technique made it possible for me to read books that were more advanced than my current reading ability.

My mom also took me to the eye doctor. According to my optometrist, I had both dyslexia and something called ocular motor dysfunction, or OMD for short. The OMD meant that my eyes were not working together as

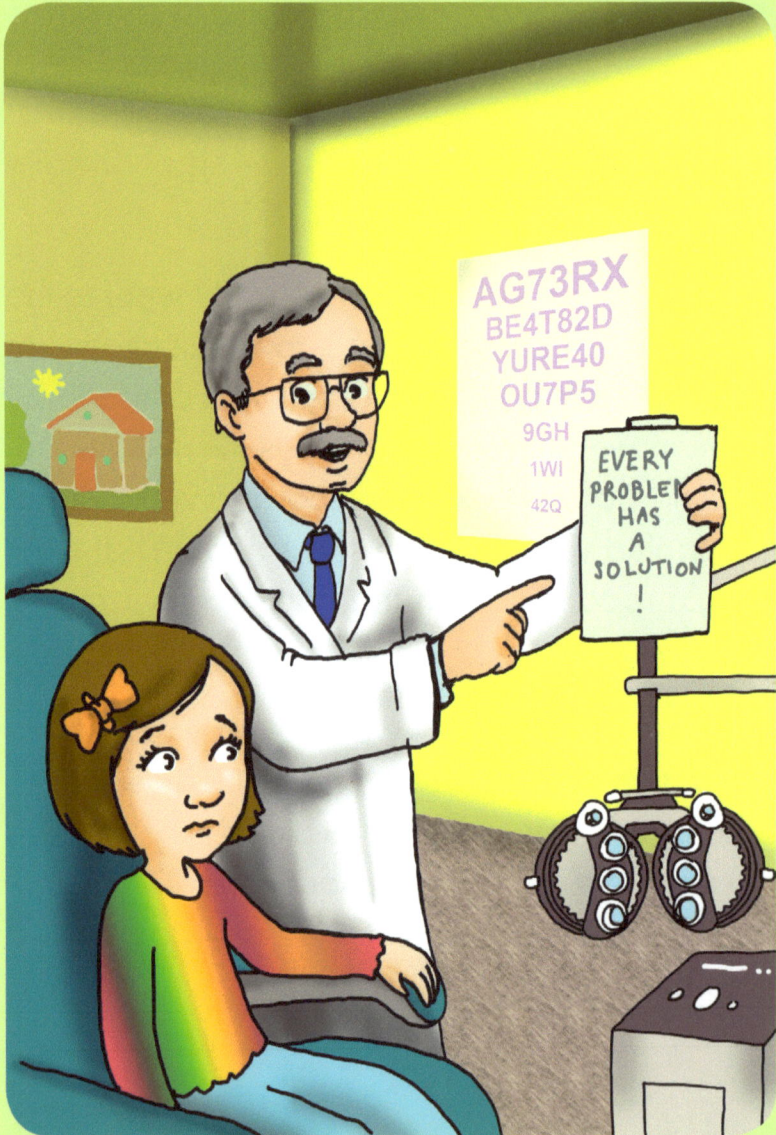

a team and therefore were struggling to track quickly from one word to the next. The eye doctor said that vision therapy would help with that.

The vision therapist taught me a helpful trick during one of our weekly sessions: to avoid skipping lines of text, I underlined words with my finger to keep my place. My optometrist also encouraged me to use a colored plastic ruler to guide my eyes when reading so I would not lose my place.

The colored ruler and the finger trick worked, but they also made me feel embarrassed and stupid. No one else in my class had to read with special rulers. I thought that using these reading aids made it obvious to other people that I had

trouble reading. I did not want to stand out anymore than I already did. When I was called on to read aloud in class throughout elementary and middle school, the other kids often snickered and teased me because I read so slowly.

To make my dyslexia less noticeable, I developed my own tricks. I read with my face close to the materials. I also kept my thumb on the edge of the page, marking the line I was reading. After I read every single word in a line, I moved my thumb down to the next line.

I also learned how to "skim read," an extremely helpful trick when it comes to finding information for a homework assignment. In skim reading, you read through something as fast as you can to get an overview of the information and major ideas. Then you go back and read it again more thoroughly. Using skim reading, I was able to read ahead in my classes. Being familiar with the text made it less likely that I would stumble over my words when teachers called on me.

I continued reading along with books on tape until I reached the fifth grade. By that time, I was reading two

to three books a week at a high school level. My last book on tape was *A Separate Peace,* by John Knowles.

After that, I decided to start reading completely on my own. I began reading even faster and at a higher level. Over the years, I have accumulated a small library that currently fills two walls in my bedroom.

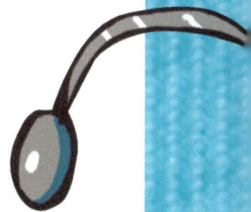

To help me build self-confidence and hone my speaking skills, my mom signed me up for a local children's theater

group. Mom was right; I did gain some confidence, not to mention a few friends along the way.

When I was twelve years old and in middle school, I found that I no longer had to struggle as much with spelling, reading, and writing as I had when I was younger. Occasionally I caught myself re-reading the same phrase or sentence. That mostly happened if I felt rushed or when I was not truly concentrating on what I was reading.

My math skills continued to improve, too. When I took my time and re-read the questions, I could easily solve

the complicated problems. It was the basic ones that still tripped me up, usually because I tried to go too fast.

Today, I am in high school. I have become so good at reading despite my brain-based disability that many people are surprised when I tell them I have dyslexia. They look at me slack-jawed. "But you do so well in school!" they say. "Aren't dyslexic people just lazy or stupid?"

That makes me angry, but I answer calmly. I know they just don't understand, so I teach them what I know, which is that dyslexia is a neurological disorder that makes it

difficult for even smart people to read. Dyslexia does not mean lazy and stupid...or careless, incompetent, or unable to concentrate.

Some of the most brilliant, accomplished, and focused people throughout history have struggled with dyslexia: inventors and scientists like Thomas Edison, Alexander Graham Bell, and Sir Isaac Newton; Nobel prizewinners like Albert Einstein; political figures like Winston Churchill; and artists and architects like Leonardo da Vinci, to name a few. The list goes on and on and on.

Sometimes people think I'm lying when I say I have dyslexia because I do so well in school, even in all the hard classes. Or they say, "I'd never know it."

I no longer hide it or feel ashamed of being different. I say, "Yes, I still have dyslexia, but I have learned how to lessen its influence. I don't let it hold me back."

Once we learn ways to compensate for our atypical brains, those of us with dyslexia aren't that easy to spot. At first, we try to blend in because we don't like feeling different; we're embarrassed to let others know we have a learning disability. Eventually, we blend in because we find ways to read and comprehend what we read. We still have a learning disability, but we don't let it stop us from learning.

Having dyslexia just means I have to work extra hard, and ALWAYS double-check my work for mistakes.

There is no medication for dyslexia. It cannot be cured by a quick trip to the doctor or with a magic pill. However, dyslexic people can succeed. They can accomplish anything that people without dyslexia can accomplish.

Today, I am dyslexic. I will always be dyslexic. I will continue to struggle. But I am not going to let dyslexia stop me from being the best person I can be.

Millions of people have found, with the help of their families, friends, and teachers, that dyslexia might slow them down, but it can never stop them. And soon those letters and numbers look less like Greek and start to unscramble themselves.

Photograph by Laura Fay

Kelly Fay is a high school student in southwest Florida. She loves reading, writing, poetry, art museums, theater, and swimming. She's not too fond of spelling or math, but strives everyday to improve her skills. She believes that anyone living with dyslexia is brave and magical. For more information about Kelly Fay and her stories, visit her website, www.kellyfay.com.

www.ingramcontent.com/pod-product-compliance
Lightning Source LLC
Chambersburg PA
CBHW040348060426
42445CB00030B/156